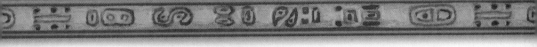

NATIONAL GEOGRAPHIC **OUR WORLD**

COYOTE'S WEEKEND

BASED ON COYOTE MAYA FOLKTALES

BY RUBEN GARCIA

NATIONAL GEOGRAPHIC LEARNING

CENGAGE Learning

Every Saturday morning, Coyote goes hiking. This morning, it is hot and sunny. Coyote puts food in his backpack.

"After I go hiking, I can go on a picnic," says Coyote.

Coyote goes hiking. He hikes all morning.

At lunchtime, he sits next to a big rock. He takes out the food for his picnic.

Rabbit sees Coyote's food. Rabbit wants the food.

Rabbit shouts, "Coyote! Help!
This big rock is going to fall on us!"
Coyote runs to help Rabbit.

Coyote holds the rock, but it really isn't falling.
Rabbit is tricking Coyote.

"Hold the rock," says Rabbit. "I'll get help!"

But Rabbit doesn't get help. He takes
Coyote's food!

Poor Coyote.

The next day is Sunday. It is a quiet afternoon.
Coyote is going fishing. He takes his best fishing rod.
He wants to catch lots of fish.

Coyote fishes all day long. He catches many fish and builds a fire to cook them.

Rabbit comes to the pond to go swimming.

"That's a lot of fish!" says Rabbit.

"They're all for me!" says Coyote.

"You know what tastes great with fish?"
says Rabbit. "Cheese!"
"Cheese?" asks Coyote.
"Yes!" says Rabbit. "And look! There's
a giant piece of cheese in the water."

Rabbit points to something big
and round in the water.
Is it cheese?
No! It's the moon shining on the water.
Rabbit is tricking Coyote again!

"How can I get the cheese?" asks Coyote.

"First you have to get all the water out of the pond," says Rabbit. "The cheese is under the water."

Coyote starts drinking the water.

Soon, all the water is gone from the pond. It is now in Coyote. But there is no cheese!

Rabbit takes Coyote's fish. Coyote can't stop him. He is too full to move!

Poor Coyote.

Facts About Weekend Volunteering

What do you do on the weekend? Maybe you like to visit friends, go hiking, or go swimming. But have you ever thought about volunteering? To volunteer means to do things for free to help others.

Here are some of the ways you can volunteer on the weekend.

Work on a mural to make your town more beautiful.

Plant trees.

Clean up a beach.

Read books to young children.

What ways can you volunteer on the weekend?

Fun with
Weekend Activities

What is each child going to do?

| go fishing | go on a picnic | go swimming | go hiking |

1. _go on a picnic_ 3. _____

2. _____ 4. _____

Match each activity with three things people use for the activity.

go fishing

go hiking

go swimming

What activities do you do on the weekend? What things do you bring with you for each activity? Use a bilingual dictionary if necessary.

Glossary

backpack a bag that you wear on your back

beach a place with a lot of sand next to an ocean, lake, or pond

fishing rod a long stick with a line that is used to catch fish

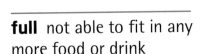

full not able to fit in any more food or drink

mural a big picture painted on the side of a building

shining sending light onto something

tricking making someone believe something that is not true